the universe in 57 words

SEVEN DAYS INSIDE THE LORD'S PRAYER

CAROLYN ARENDS

Copyright © 2021 Carolyn Arends
All rights reserved.
Pubished in the United States by Renovaré.

Unless otherwise noted, Scripture quotations are from New Revised Standard Version Bible, copyright © 1989 National Council of the Churches of Christ in the United States of America. Used by permission. All rights reserved worldwide.

Our Father which art in heaven,
Hallowed be thy name.
Thy kingdom come,
Thy will be done in earth,
As it is in heaven.
Give us this day our daily bread.
And forgive us our debts,
As we forgive our debtors.
And lead us not into temptation,
But deliver us from evil.
For thine is the kingdom,
And the power, and the glory,
For ever. Amen.

Matthew 6:9–13, KJV

INTRODUCTION

I can recall rattling through the Lord's Prayer—and singing "God Save the Queen"—as a Canadian kid in public school. (Those memories seem surreal in today's post-Christian Canada.) Even though I was already developing a prayer life of my own, the Lord's Prayer seemed archaic and starchy. I was oblivious to the power and beauty within the words I mumbled.

Now I know better.

When Jesus' friends asked him how they should pray, he gave them—and us—the brilliantly succinct guide we call the "Lord's Prayer." In a feat of cosmic engineering, Jesus managed to gather the entire waterfront of human need and the vast ocean of God's plans for his universe in just 57 Greek words. We can pray those 57 words (or their English equivalents) for a lifetime and never exhaust them.

AN INTENTIONAL JOURNEY

However well acquainted you are with the Lord's Prayer, I invite you to use this booklet to go on a seven-part journey into the heart of the Trinity. Each section consists of a reading, a reflective prayer exercise, and a suggested song. You may wish to take a section a day and live inside the prayer for a week. Or you may prefer to savor your exploration and take seven weeks . . . or seven months.

Whatever timing you choose, let's take a moment to look at the prayer as a whole before we begin.

THREE GIFTS

Far from a hollow ritual, the prayer is freighted with remarkable gifts.

A Road Map

The Lord's Prayer consists of an invocation and six brief petitions. To pray these petitions in the order Jesus gives them is to travel from the way we view the world to the way God sees it. In N. T. Wright's insightful language, these petitions move us "from paranoia to prayer" and "from fuss to faith."[1]

The prayer is so expansive, so aligned with God's heart for his world, that it establishes the terrain for all other prayers. If we find ourselves praying something counter to the Lord's Prayer, we're heading off the map.

That's not to say we should stifle even our most wrong-headed prayers. Whatever is in our hearts must be prayed out or left to fester. But as we pray things out in the company of Jesus, we will find that our longings gradually migrate into the territory of the Lord's Prayer. To quote a tongue twister from P. T. Forsythe, "Petitions that are less than pure are only purified by petitions."

The petitions in the Lord's Prayer are landmarks by which we can orient our prayers and our lives.

A Window

Even better than a road map, the Lord's Prayer is a window into the very heart of God. In a world of injustice, poverty, bitterness, and evil, Jesus teaches us to pray for justice, bread, forgiveness, and deliverance. To pray this prayer is to discover what the Father, Son, and Spirit really care about.

An Invitation to Causality

In teaching us the Lord's Prayer, Jesus offers us a thrilling invitation to participate in God's ongoing plan to redeem and restore all things. Embedded in this prayer is the conviction that praying it somehow changes the course of history. The Lord's Prayer gives us "the dignity of causality."[2]

Exactly how our prayers and God's plans intermingle is incomprehensible. But Jesus assures us that our lives and prayers truly make a difference. New Testament scholar George Beasley-Murray writes,

> It would seem that God has willed that the prayers of his people should be part of the process by which the kingdom comes. The interaction between the sovereignty of God and the prayers of the saints is part of the ultimate mystery of existence. Faith is called on to take both seriously.[3]

POWERFUL COSMIC ACTION

To pray the Lord's Prayer is to participate in the transformation of the world. But we should acknowledge at the outset that there are times when that transformation is barely perceptible to the naked eye.

It might help us to think of the Crab Nebula—an exploding star in the constellation Taurus.[4] If you peer at this supernova through a telescope, it looks like a colorful smudge. Photographs taken from earth of the Crab Nebula fifteen years ago will look identical to images taken today.

But here's the thing. Every day the Crab Nebula expands by 70 million miles. Powerful, explosive, cosmic action is taking place all the time, but it's imperceptible from our perspective.

Jesus teaches us that something similar is going on when we pray. Sometimes, the answers to our prayers are swift and obvious. Other times, nothing much seems to be happening from our vantage point. Either way, powerful, explosive, cosmic action is taking place.

The Trinity's radiant, consuming, transforming love is blazing at the center of the universe. And Jesus is inviting us in.

A WORD ABOUT TRANSLATIONS, TITLES, PRONOUNS, AND SOURCES

I have chosen to express the petitions primarily in the words of the King James Version, as that is the translation of the Lord's Prayer that many of us know by heart. All other Scripture quotations are taken from the New Revised Standard Version.

It's worth mentioning that the "Lord's Prayer" is a bit of a misnomer. The prayers found in Matthew 6 and Luke 11 might be better titled the "Disciple's Prayer," while the intimate prayer captured between Jesus and his Father in John 17 is more truly the Lord's own prayer. Still, I continue to refer to the former as the "Lord's Prayer," as that is the title most familiar to us.

Because the image of God as Father is so important to this prayer, I've elected to retain the traditional masculine pronouns for the Trinity throughout this resource. We should always keep in mind, though, that while the Incarnate Son is indeed a man, the Triune God is neither male nor female; and any gender-based language we employ for the Godhead is analogical.

This resource has been influenced by more authors, preachers, teachers, and fellow pray-ers than I can credit or even remember. But I am particularly indebted to the following works: *Fifty-Seven Words That Change the World*, by Darrell Johnson; *The Lord and His Prayer*, by N. T. Wright; *The Divine Conspiracy*, by Dallas Willard; *Prayer*, by Richard Foster; and Eugene Peterson's "Jesus and Prayer" lectures for SPIR 604 at Regent College.

You will note that for each day's exploration there is a suggested song. To access the songs, visit **renovare.org/universesongs**.

After this manner therefore pray ye . . .

(Pray then in this way . . .)

DAY ONE
THE INVOCATION

Our Father which art in heaven . . .

The first thing Jesus teaches us is an invocation—pointing us toward the right address, in multiple senses of the word.

Whom are we addressing? *Our Father*
Where is his address? *In heaven*

Dallas Willard argues that "addressing God is what distinguishes prayer from worrying out loud."[5] As soon as I speak or even think the opening words of the Lord's Prayer, I'm pulled out of my internal echo chamber and into a two-way conversation.

Jesus could have taught us to address THE GREAT I AM or THE LORD MOST HIGH. Instead, he invites us to use highly relational, parental language. If God is *Our Father*, then we are *his children*. Fathers—good ones, anyway—are accessible to their kids and delight in giving them good things.

It's worth pausing here to reflect on how our earthly dads color the canvas of our picture of God as father. Especially for those with father wounds, the image is easily distorted. Thankfully, Jesus shows us the heavenly Father in his person and in his parables.

Picture the father in the parable of the prodigal son. There is nothing a wayward child can do to "unfather" that father; it's impossible to change his character or out-sin his love. This, Jesus tells us, is the kind of father to whom we pray.

Do you see the beautiful efficiency of the Lord's Prayer so far? It takes Jesus only two words to reveal something seismic about the heart of God and his desire to act for our good. And with those same two words, he gives us our own identity in the equation. We're not needy, anonymous blips in an indifferent universe. Rather, we are needy, beloved children of a God who takes fatherly delight in caring for us.

Addressing God as *Our Father* gives us the basis for all the petitions to follow, because it assures us that God has the *desire* to act on our behalf. But how do we know that God also has the *power* to act? This is where the second part of the address comes in.

"The LORD has established his throne in the heavens," writes the psalmist in Psalm 103:19, "and his kingdom rules over all." By teaching us to pray to "Our Father *in heaven*," Jesus is reminding us that the God we are addressing is on his throne and in charge of the universe.

Yet even as God's heavenly address reminds us of his sovereignty and transcendence, it also assures us of his proximity and immanence. The biblical writers pictured the heavens not as a remote location but as the dimension where God reigns—the invisible realm that extends far beyond the farthest galaxy, but is also as near as the atmosphere surrounding our bodies.

Our Father which art in heaven. With this brief address, Jesus gives us "the configuration of the reality from within which we pray."[6]

THREE IMPLICATIONS OF THE INVOCATION

We need to recapture a bit of the shock that Jesus' first students would have experienced when they heard this address. They were likely startled on at least three fronts.

Intimacy

First, Jesus signals an astonishing level of access to God. We know Jesus addressed God as *Abba*—an Aramaic word that carries perhaps a touch more respect than the English term *daddy*, but no less tenderness. In teaching us to pray *Our Father*, Jesus is inviting us into that same sort of intimacy with the God of the universe.

For Jesus' first listeners—Jews who had been taught all sorts of prohibitions related to addressing God with the proper reverence—the invitation to address him as "Father" or "Abba" must have been mind-boggling. Something about the way humans are able to relate to God has shifted dramatically, and it has everything to do with Jesus.

Theologian Baxter Kruger tells a story that cracks open a bit of the miracle on offer. Baxter was in his office one Saturday afternoon when his young son and a playmate appeared, decked out in camouflage, evidently embroiled in a game of *Army*. "My son peers around the corner of the door and looks at me," Kruger remembers, "and the next thing I know, he comes flying through the air and jumps on me. We start wrestling and horsing around and we end up on the floor. Then his buddy flies into us and all three of us are just like a wad of laughter."

In the middle of their play, Kruger felt the Lord prompting him to pay attention. He realized he'd never met his son's friend before. "I re-wound the story and thought about what would have happened if this little boy would have walked into my den alone. . . . Would he fly through the air and engage me in play? . . . Of course not. That is the last thing that would have happened."

"Within himself," Kruger continues, "that little boy had no freedom to have a relationship with me. We were strangers.... The miracle that happened was that my son's knowledge of my acceptance and delight, and my son's freedom for fellowship with me, rubbed off onto that other little boy.... He participated in my son's life and communion with me."[7]

When Jesus invites us to call *his* Father *our* Father, he is offering us intimate participation in the life of the Trinity.

Community

In the invocation, Jesus teaches that our connection to God is *very personal*, yet it is also *not private*. The address, after all, is not *My* Father, but *Our* Father. And all the personal pronouns that follow in the prayer are plural.

From the *first word* of the prayer forward, Jesus invites us to begin to understand our story within the context of a much bigger story. To pray this prayer is to find our individual lives situated within the body of Christ, within humanity, and within all of creation.

Vocation

There is a third, rather cosmic dimension of the invocation that is easy to overlook unless we receive Jesus' teaching in the context of Israel's backstory. N. T. Wright points out that the first occurrence of the idea of God as "Father" comes during the dramatic scene, captured in Exodus 4, when Moses thunders to Pharaoh on the Lord's behalf: "Thus says the Lord: Israel is my firstborn son.... Let my son go that he may worship me" (Exodus 4:22–23).

From that iconic confrontation forward, to refer to God as "Father" is associated in the Jewish mind with the promise of liberation—freedom from slavery and oppression. By the time King David comes along, God is explaining that eventually there will be a new king, a Messiah, descended from David's family—and the God-as-Father motif continues. "I will be a father to him," he says of the promised Messiah, "and he shall be a son to me" (2 Samuel 7:14).

When Jesus arrives on the scene, Israel has been waiting for this Davidic Messiah, the hope of Israel, for a very long time. They've suffered under the oppression of one regime after another, longing for the day when their Lord, Yahweh, will enact a new exodus and finally set his people free. When Jesus starts referring to God as his "Father," it's a signal, loud and clear, that he is claiming to be the long-awaited emancipator.

And then, do you see what he does? It would be one thing if he taught his followers to pray to *his* Father. But instead, he teaches us to pray to *our* Father—which is to include *ourselves* in the mission.

Right here, in the invocation, Jesus is inviting all who will pray this prayer to self-identify as participants in the Father's great project of setting every captive free and overcoming evil with good in every corner of the universe. To pray to "*our* Father" is to find our life's ultimate vocation. It is to sign up for the revolution.

And our participation in this revolution means that we are invited to embody God's kingdom everywhere we go—at home, at work, at church, shopping for groceries, posting on social media, interacting with our neighbors. We're invited to live aware and expectant—growing in our capacity to detect all the subtle and overt ways the people around us experience oppression, and learning to pray and act for their liberation.

When I look back on my church upbringing, I'm grateful there was a strong emphasis on the possibility of a personal, intimate relationship with God. But I must confess that I somehow missed the communal, cosmic, revolutionary side of the beautiful coin Jesus offers us.

"Spiritual depth and renewal come, as and when they come, as part of the larger package," observes N. T. Wright. "But that package itself is about being delivered from evil; about God's kingdom coming on earth as it is in heaven."[8]

> ***Whom are we addressing?*** *Our Father*
> ***Where is his address?*** *In heaven*
> ***Where is OUR address?*** *Intimately centered in the life of the Trinity, communally situated within the body of Christ and all of creation, and thrillingly placed on the frontlines of the revolution.*

Suggested song: "Who You Are"
renovare.org/universesongs

LIVING INSIDE THE INVOCATION

Is there an aspect of the invocation—intimacy, community, or vocation—to which the Holy Spirit is drawing your attention? You are invited to center your conversation with God in one or more of those areas.

Intimacy
- When you pray to God as "Father," are you picturing the Father whom Jesus described? Read through the Parable of the Prodigal Son and ask God to reveal himself more deeply as the one who runs to you while you are still a long way off.
- What does this level of intimacy and access mean for the burdens that most concern you today?

Community
- When you pray to God as "*Our* Father," you are invited to move from individualism to an awareness of:
  - Your place in the body of Christ
  - God's love for all of humankind
  - God's purposes for all of creation
- How does this awareness of being part of a cosmic community shape the burdens that most concern you today?

Vocation
- When you pray to God as "Our Father," you are invited to say yes to being a co-revolutionary in bringing about God's kingdom. How might this affect your attitude and behavior in relation to your home? Your school? Your workplace? Your church? Your city? Your country?

DAY TWO
PETITION ONE

Hallowed be thy name ... in earth, as it is in heaven.

A man I met on a plane told me a story. He and his wife, a piano major at a local university, went piano shopping. The saleswoman led them straight to the entry-level models. "She had us pegged exactly right," the man told me. "We were going to have to borrow the money to get the cheapest instrument there."

Everything changed, however, when the name of the prospective buyer's mentor—a world-renowned master teaching at the university—came up in their conversation. The saleswoman was panic-stricken. "Not these pianos!" she exclaimed, herding the couple away from the economy section and into a private showroom of gleaming Steinways. "I'm so sorry," she kept repeating, horrified at the thought of the teacher finding out she'd shown one of his students an inferior instrument. Try as they might, they couldn't persuade her to take them back to the pianos they could afford. Once the master's name came up, only the best would do.

When I think about the reverence that flustered saleswoman had for a teacher's name, Jesus' first petition begins to come to focus.

REVERENCE ... AND REVELATION

What does it mean to "hallow" God's name? Maybe you, like me, were raised to flinch whenever someone uses God's name as a mindless exclamation or curse. Perhaps you've heard about the extreme care taken in some branches of Judaism: Pages containing *Yahweh*, the covenantal name of the Lord, are never thoughtlessly discarded, but rather buried or ritually burned. When we pray this first petition, we're invited to cultivate reverence for God's name—especially while living in a world prone to profane it.

But as important as it is to use God's name with care, if we live inside this first petition for long we'll begin to see that Jesus is inviting us not only to cultivate reverence, but to pray for revelation.

Names are a big deal in the Bible. From Abraham ("Father of Many") to Jacob ("Heel-grasper") to Peter ("Rock"), monikers don't merely identify—they reveal. Moses understood this. So he asked God (whom he knew by the generic deity designation *Elohim*) for his personal name. "Yahweh," God told him, offering Moses the kind of intimacy that only comes on a first-name basis—and revealing his covenant with his people in the process.

As we learned from the invocation, every name we have for God is a revelation of his character. So when Jesus teaches us to pray for the hallowing of God's name, he's really teaching us to pray that God's character will be revealed here on earth, just the way it is in heaven.

Throughout Jesus' earthly ministry, he is constantly encountering people who have distorted pictures of his Father. If we pay much attention at all to his teaching in the Gospel accounts, we'll notice that more than anything he wants us to be able to see God for who God really is.

Jesus seems convinced that the coming of God's kingdom hinges on the hallowing of God's name—the revealing of God's character. He knows that we become like the God we worship, and if our God-picture is distorted, then the more religious we become, the worse off we will be. So the first, foundational thing Jesus teaches us to pray for is a clear revelation of God's character. Tom Smith helpfully translates *hallowed be thy name* as "help us draw healing pictures of You."

ONLY GOD CAN DO IT

None of the six petitions Jesus teaches us are things we can obtain on our own. In fact, the verbs in two of the first three petitions are imperative, but passive. This means that this first request is not so much "Let us hallow your name" as it is "Father, do what we can't—make your name holy throughout the earth."

Only God can reveal himself to the world. But if we pray as he taught us, our reverence and care for his name will grow, right alongside our capacity to behold God's goodness and beauty. Which gets me thinking about that piano saleswoman again. Because the more we see the glory of God's love, the more we'll begin to exchange our cheap instruments of self-interest and power for the costly cross of Christ—the only instrument worthy of our master's name.

> Suggested song: "All Hail the Power of Jesus' Name"
> *renovare.org/universesongs*

LIVING INSIDE THE FIRST PETITION

Darrell Johnson suggests that one of the ways we can enter into the prayer "Hallowed be thy name" is to "pray back" the names of God in terms of what they reveal about his character.[9] For example, Darrell suggests that we might "pray back" the name *El Shaddai* like this: "Oh Father, you are *El Shaddai*, the Mighty One. Make yourself real as the Mighty One in my life as it is in heaven."

Or we might "pray back" the name *Good Shepherd* like this: "Oh Father, my neighbors are having a hard time. Please make yourself real to them as the *Shepherd* who carries his sheep; enhance your reputation as the *Good Shepherd* in my apartment building."

Read over the following names for God. If one or two of the names particularly catch your attention, meditate on the related Scriptures and then "pray them back." Consider writing out your prayers, as you invite God to hallow his name the way only he can.

Abba – Rom. 8:15

Advocate – 1 John 2:1

Almighty – Rev. 1:8

Alpha & Omega – Rev. 21:6

Author & Perfecter of our Faith – Heb. 12:2

Bread of Life – John 6:35, 48

Comforter – 2 Cor. 1:3–5

Cornerstone – 1 Peter 2:7–8

Creator – Isa. 40:28

Deliverer – Rom. 11:26

El Roi (The God Who Sees) – Gen. 16:13

Emmanuel – Matt. 1:23

Everlasting Father – Isa. 9:6

Friend of Sinners – Matt. 11:19

Gate for the Sheep – John 10:7

Good Shepherd – John 10:11

High Priest – Heb. 3:1

King of Kings – 1 Tim. 6:15; Rev. 19:16

Lamb of God – John 1:29

Life – John 11:25

Light of the World – John 8:12; 9:5

Lion – Rev. 5:5

Living Water – John 7:37–38

Lord of Lords – Rev. 19:16

Love – 1 John 4:8

Mediator – 1 Tim. 2:5

Messiah – John 4:25–26

Morning Star – Rev. 22:16

Peace – Eph. 2:13–15

Physician – Matt. 9:12

Ransom – 1 Tim. 2:6

Redeemer – Isa. 41:14

Refiner – Mal. 3:2

Refuge – Isa. 25:4

Resurrection – John 11:25

Righteousness – Jer. 23:6

Rock – Deut. 32:4

Ruler of God's Creation – Rev. 3:14

Sacrifice – Eph. 5:2

Savior – 2 Sam. 22:47; Luke 1:47

Servant – Isa. 42:1

Truth – John 14:6

Way – John 14:6

Wonderful Counselor – Isa. 9:6

Word – John 1:1

Vine – John 15:5

DAY THREE
PETITION TWO

Thy kingdom come ... in earth, as it is in heaven.

If we're going to pray "Thy kingdom come," we're going to need to understand what Jesus means by *kingdom*.

HOW JESUS DESCRIBES HIS GOSPEL

Jesus' public ministry began with his proclamation, "Repent, for the kingdom of heaven has come near" (Matthew 4:17).

Once again, we hear Jesus using prophetic language unmistakable to the Jewish ear, signalling that he is the fulfillment of long-awaited promises. But if the kingdom "has come near" in Matthew 4, why does Jesus teach us to pray for it to come in Matthew 6? It will help us to look closely at four key words in Matthew 4:17—*repent*, *kingdom*, *heaven*, and *near*.

Repent
For any of us who grew up in the hot, scary shadows of brimstone pulpits, the command *to repent* causes an involuntary shudder. But the Greek word is *metanoeo*, which is more invitation than threat. It means "to change your mind," or "to reconsider."

Reconsider what? According to Jesus, everything you thought you knew about reality. Why? Because the kingdom of heaven is near.

Kingdom

A *kingdom,* Dallas Willard points out, is a region where a ruler has domain—the place where whatever he or she wants done, gets done. God's kingdom, then, is "the range of his effective will"—the place where what God wants done comes to pass.[10]

Thus, God's kingdom is the invisible but very real realm where God reigns, and it's characterized by love, truth, justice, goodness, and wholeness. It's a wonderful place to be. The apostle Paul testifies that "the kingdom of God is . . . righteousness and peace and joy in the Holy Spirit" (Romans 14:17).

Heaven

While Jesus often speaks of the "kingdom of God," in Matthew's Gospel we find him emphasizing that this kingdom is also the "kingdom of *heaven.*"

Most of us think of heaven as somewhere "out there," the place where God watches from a distance and we will one day join him. But for the biblical writers, heaven is close. The "first heavens" is a term used to describe the earth's atmosphere. So when Jesus describes the invisible realm that God inhabits, he lets us know it's not only "out there," but also as near as the atmosphere surrounding our bodies. God's kingdom is so close that "in him we live and move and have our being" (Acts 17:28).

Near

When Jesus says that the kingdom *has come near*, he is announcing the incredible news that God's kingdom is now accessible in a new way. In Jesus' first recorded words in Mark's Gospel, he prefaces this announcement with the dramatic phrase "The time is fulfilled" (1:15). The implication is that with Christ's earthly arrival, history has reached a crisis point. Everything has changed. The kingdom of heaven has begun to break into earthly existence like never before. As Trevor Hudson likes to say, Jesus is now announcing the availability of another kind of life.

But here's the rub. As real and available as God's kingdom is, there are still, for now, competing kingdoms. In fact, part of what makes us human is the fact that each one of us has a personal kingdom—"a realm," Willard says, "that is uniquely our own, where our choice determines what happens."[11] We always have the option to align our little kingdoms either with God's kingdom or with the kingdoms of this world.

That's why, with this second petition of the Lord's Prayer, Jesus teaches us to pray for the kingdom to come more fully into our lives, our neighborhoods, our churches, our governments, every corner of our world—until God's reign is as complete in us as it is in heaven. We're asking him to supplant the competing kingdoms that operate in our individual hearts and in our collective systems. And once again, we're asking God to do what only he can do.

There is, of course, a dissonance we sometimes feel between the peace and wholeness of God's kingdom and the discord and death of this world. Chris Hall calls this an "Overlap of the Ages"—we live in this Present Evil Age even as we begin to participate in the Age to Come.

What should we do when we experience this dissonance—when we find ourselves "groan[ing] inwardly while we wait for adoption, the redemption of our bodies" (Romans 8:23)? According to Jesus, we should pray for the kingdom to come, trusting that God is incorporating our prayers and lives in his ongoing mission to restore and redeem all things.

Suggested song: "We Come"
renovare.org/universesongs

LIVING INSIDE THE SECOND PETITION

Make a list of the kingdoms you encounter every day.

Some of the kingdoms under your control may include your inner thought life; your financial choices; what you eat and drink; your social media use; and, to an extent, the running of your household.

Some of the kingdoms out of your control may include your extended family; the operation of your local, regional, and national governments, systems of education, and justice; and the various competing value systems in the wider culture.

As you consider all the kingdoms that overlap with your life (both those under your control and out of your control), do you notice an area for which you are currently carrying a burden? If so, spend some time simply lifting up that zone into God's light and love, asking for his kingdom to come.

You may or may not emerge with a clearer sense of how you might participate in God's mission in that area. In any case, time spent asking for the kingdom to come is never wasted.

DAY FOUR
PETITION THREE

Thy will be done ... in earth, as it is in heaven.

The third petition that Jesus teaches us flows naturally out of the second. When we begin to see what it means for God's kingdom to come, why *wouldn't* we want the effective range of his will to extend further and further throughout the earth?

Lisa Koons, a leader in the 24/7 prayer movement, was asked how Christians could possibly pray together during a divisive political season. "We pray sweeping prayers, prayers we can agree on, while leaving the outcome to God," Lisa answered. Even if we have very different theories about what God's will might look like in a given situation, our hearts can be united in our desire for his will to be done.

So Jesus gives us a compact petition that can embrace every need, every longing, every complex issue, even our disparate ways of seeing the world: *Thy will be done.*

HOW DO WE KNOW GOD'S WILL?

Years ago, I toured as an opening act for Rich Mullins.[12] There was something about Rich's music that stirred up people's deepest longings. I loved overhearing conversations at the autograph table; they often turned serious and urgent.

More than once, a fan asked Rich how to discern the will of God.

Rich would listen, and then offer an unexpected perspective.

"I don't think finding God's plan for you has to be complicated," he'd begin. "God's will is that you love him with all your heart and soul and mind, and also that you love your neighbor as yourself. Get busy with that, and then, if God wants you to do something unusual, he'll take care of it. Say, for example, he wants you to go to Egypt." Rich would pause for a moment before flashing his trademark grin. "If that's the case, he'll provide eleven jealous brothers and they'll sell you into slavery."

When I find myself wrestling with life decisions, I think of Rich's Egypt Principle. It makes me laugh, and then it asks me to get down to the serious business of determining which of my options allows me to best love God and other people. Such an approach reminds me, once again, that my life with God is personal but never private. It usually rules out certain possibilities, while affirming—even creating—several others.

Sometimes, once I've narrowed down my alternatives in light of the Great Commandment to love God and other people, the determinative "jealous brothers" do show up. A scholarship comes through at one school and not another. A job offer is escalated or rescinded. Other times, however, I'm left standing at the junction of several seemingly reasonable pathways, miserable with uncertainty. If only Rich were around to dispatch further wisdom!

It's when I reach those loggerheads that I am once again grateful for the passive, imperative verbs Jesus teaches us. Ultimately, the third petition is much less "Tell me your will so I can do it" than it is "Please do your will in me."

What's more, as helpful as this prayer is when I don't know what to do, it's even more essential when I *do* know what God is asking of me, but I'm unable to align my will with his. "Even when you can't be willing to do what God is asking," a friend often reminds me, "you can be willing to be willing." The third petition invites me to move from a position of willfulness to willingness, giving God an opening to begin to complete his will in me in the way only he can.

HOW DO WE LIVE GOD'S WILL?

The Jesus who teaches us to pray the third petition is, of course, its perfect model. "My food," he once told his disciples, "is to do the will of him who sent me and to complete his work" (John 4:34).

It's worth noting that Jesus' way of doing his Father's will often seemed to defy productivity models and baffle his disciples. He seldom took the fastest way anywhere, preferring circuitous routes that gave him more time on the road with his friends. He was eminently interruptible, particularly by children and outcasts. And he had a tendency to slip away at seemingly inopportune moments to pray.

It's a tragedy, Eugene Peterson used to say, when we end up doing "Jesus things" in a way that Jesus would never do them. More than once I've participated in an evangelistic event where the behind-the-scenes volunteers were treated like cogs in a machine. We've all seen debates over right doctrine turn ugly. And I wince when I remember the times I let my graduate studies in theology—a path on which I was clear Jesus was leading me—turn into an obsessive quest for grades at the expense of time with my family.

So as we pray this third petition, it's important to remember we are asking for God's will to be done not only in *what* we do, but also in *how* we do it. We're asking the Holy Spirit to teach us how to do Jesus things in the Jesus way.

> Suggested song: "Father, Thy Will Be Done"
> *renovare.org/universesongs*

LIVING INSIDE THE THIRD PETITION

Are you aware of an area in which your will is not aligned with God's? If you're finding it difficult to surrender, consider telling God that you are willing to be willing.

You may wish to use the Palms Down, Palms Up Prayer[13] in this process.

Find a comfortable place to sit. Take a few minutes (and a few deep breaths) to center yourself and become aware of God's loving presence.

Imagine that you are holding the matter of concern in your hands. Clench your fists to represent any tension you feel around this issue.

Then, as a symbol of your willingness (rather than your ability) to surrender this matter, open your hands and place your palms down on your lap. Pray as honestly as you can, perhaps something like: *Lord, I am not yet able to fully let this go. But I am willing to be willing. I am relinquishing the idea that I can do this on my own, and turning my inability to surrender over to you.*

When you feel ready, turn your palms upward to indicate your willingness to receive from God. Again, keep your prayers honest: *Only you can give me the grace and growth I need to be able to surrender. I am open to receiving what you have for me, in your perfect time.*

You may need to pray this Palms Down, Palms Up Prayer many times, over many days, but don't lose hope. God is much more patient than we are.

DAY FIVE
PETITION FOUR

Give us this day our ***daily bread.***

The phrase *in earth, as it is in heaven* acts as a fulcrum in the middle of the Lord's prayer. The first three petitions keep us focused squarely on God—his name, his kingdom, his will. We pray that heaven may increasingly invade our earthly experience.

Now, with our hearts and minds calibrated Godward, Jesus invites us to lift up our earthly needs—for sustenance, for forgiveness, and for deliverance—to our Father in heaven.

It starts here: *Give us this day our daily bread.*

WHAT DOES JESUS MEAN BY "DAILY BREAD"?

Once again, we see Jesus' genius for packing a universe of meaning into a single phrase. At least four implications can be teased out of this request for "daily bread."

Basic Needs
The Greek word that gets translated as "daily" in the Lord's Prayer is *epiousios*. It's a peculiar term not found in any other Greek literature or any part of the Bible other than the Lord's Prayer. Its exact meaning has been debated for centuries. Is Jesus talking about actual bread? Or is he employing a purely spiritual metaphor? Given that *ousious* means "sustenance" and *epi* is an intensifier, we might

say that Jesus is referring to "super-sustenance." With that meaning in view, Origen and other early church fathers assumed that Jesus primarily had spiritual resources in mind.

Then, a century ago, an archeological dig uncovered a fifth-century Egyptian papyrus that contained several instances of the word *epiousios*. As it turns out, the papyrus was a shopping list, and the word *epiousios* was written next to a variety of grocery items.

I took a course with Eugene Peterson where he reported this discovery with an immense amount of glee. He asked us to imagine a mother sending her son to the market with the admonition, "Don't get me that day-old bread; get me the fresh stuff—the *epiousios* bread!" We can be certain, Peterson concluded, that when Jesus used that word he was referring to something as basic as the day's groceries.

So the first thing Jesus is teaching us with this petition is that we should ask God for the earthy, everyday things we need to live—from food to shelter to meaningful work and relationships. If we might wish to operate in a more spiritualized state, the fourth petition cuts through our pretensions and reminds us that we never outgrow petitionary prayer.

Not only does Jesus teach us to ask God for the basics we need to live, he urges us to do it daily. Like the Israelites who had to rely on God for manna each day, Jesus is inviting us into a rhythm of simple, steady God-dependence. The idea is not to come to him now and then, when our needs exceed our resources. It's to live every day—every hour, every minute—in a state of trusting reliance on God's provision.

For those of us who worry and plan and crave control, Jesus offers a simple training program for a different way of living. "This then," he tells us, "is how you should pray: *Give us **this** day our **daily** bread.*"

The Eucharist

With a request for "daily bread," Jesus gives us the words to ask not only for the food we need to survive physically, but also for "the bread of life" (John 6:35). "Those who eat my flesh and drink my blood have eternal life," Jesus told his disciples (John 6:54).

Then, in the upper room, he taught them how to partake. Every time we gather around the Lord's table, we're participating in one of the wondrous ways God answers the fourth petition—by giving us Jesus, the Bread of Life we need to truly live.

The Eschaton

The prophets before Jesus were fond of imagining the age to come as a lavish, sacred meal with God. So, reverberating in the request for earthly bread is a third implication—the anticipation of a wedding feast that will never end. Listen to how the vision is cast in Isaiah 25:6–8:

> On this mountain the Lord of hosts will make for all peoples
> > a feast of rich food, a feast of well-aged wines,
> > > of rich food filled with marrow, of well-aged wines
> > > > strained clear.
> And he will destroy on this mountain
> > the shroud that is cast over all peoples,

> the sheet that is spread over all nations;
> he will swallow up death forever.
> Then the Lord God will wipe away the tears from all faces,
> and the disgrace of his people he will take away from all the earth,
> for the Lord has spoken.

"Give us our daily bread," Jesus teaches us to pray, "now and forever."

Justice for the Poor
Finally, we cannot pray the fourth petition with our whole hearts without thinking about the world's poor—those who don't have enough provision for today. Once again, the Lord's Prayer draws us out of ourselves and into God's care for the world, signing us up for the revolution by inviting us to seek practical ways we can participate in the kingdom work of liberating the oppressed and feeding the hungry.

Suggested song: "Everything We Need (In the Morning, Lord)"
renovare.org/universesongs

LIVING INSIDE THE FOURTH PETITION

The petition for daily bread reminds us of our profound poverty—what Eugene Peterson calls "the condition in which we don't have what we need to live a full life." There are many layers to our poverty—and to God's willing provision. Consider praying through each of these layers, lingering on the areas where you sense the greatest need.

1. Physical bread: Basic sustenance so our bodies can operate
2. Everything necessary for functioning in the world: shelter, sleep, clothing, community, meaningful work, art, beauty, laughter, sustainable economy
3. Everything necessary for living in the kingdom: the Holy Spirit, scriptural understanding, local church community, courage, wisdom, discernment, justice, the "fruit of the Spirit"
4. Jesus himself: the Bread of Life

The petition for daily bread also reminds us of the profound poverty—material and otherwise—that exists both locally and globally. Pray through the list above again, this time with the world's hungry in view, seeking the ways in which God wants you to participate in this aspect of the coming of his kingdom.

DAY SIX
PETITION FIVE

Forgive us our debts, as we forgive our debtors.

If you're praying the Lord's Prayer with a group of people, the fifth petition is where the recitation can get a little messy. Are we asking God to forgive our "sins," our "trespasses," or our "debts"?

Each of these words gets at a different nuance of the same problem. I grew up with the "trespass" translation, and it's helped me think about the ways I violate God's loving rule. But lately I'm leaning into the language of "debt," because it hints at how entirely in hock I am to the extravagant and unmerited goodness of God. Trevor Hudson likes to pray, *Lord, I thank you that I am waking up to a day I have not made, to enjoy a salvation I have not earned.*

Greek scholars tell us that the words translated as "forgive" and "debts" in Matthew 6 are financial in nature; the petition is really a request to "clear the ledger." Imagine walking into a bank where you owed an enormous loan and requesting that your debt be erased. The fifth petition Jesus teaches us might be the boldest one yet!

NO ONE IS RIGHTEOUS

The fourth petition required us to recognize the fact that we don't have what it takes to live a full life. Now, the fifth petition acknowledges the reality that we don't have what it takes to live a righteous life.

Old Testament scholar Bruce Waltke suggests that it is helpful to think of "righteousness" as right relationship in four directions—with God, with each other, with ourselves, and with creation. All the wreckage in the world—and in our own lives—comes down to failures in loving in one or more of those relationships.

Just like regular Eucharist can help make us aware of our dependence on Jesus for all we need to live a full life, a regular practice of confession can help wake us up to our dependence on Jesus for all we need to live a righteous life.

And so Jesus bakes a frank confession into the first half of the fifth position. "Forgive us our debts," we pray, confessing them and accessing their only remedy with one simple phrase. We are beggars at the bank requesting that our ledger be wiped clean, praying with shocking boldness because Jesus said we should.

A CONTINGENT PETITION?

But what do we make of the second half of the fifth petition: "Forgive us our debts . . . *as we forgive our debtors*"? This is the only part of the Lord's Prayer that seems to be in some way contingent upon us. And it's the only petition that Jesus amplifies after instructing his followers how to pray. "For if you forgive others their trespasses, your heavenly Father will also forgive you," he declares, "but if you do not forgive others, neither will your Father forgive your trespasses" (Matthew 6:14–15).

As I've wrestled with this part of the Lord's Prayer, two things have come into focus.

A Warning against "The Secular Loop"
First, I think Jesus is cautioning us not to place ourselves in what theologian John Stackhouse calls "the secular loop." Consider the

passages earlier in Matthew 6, where Jesus warns against giving to charity or praying purely for show. In both cases, folks who have removed God from the equation and are seeking human approval have already "received their reward" (Matthew 6:2). In other words, if we want to operate solely on the human level and leave God out of it, he'll let us—at least for a while.

When we refuse to forgive, Stackhouse argues, we appoint ourselves ruler and judge, supplanting God and once again choosing to operate on a purely human level. That may be one reason why our own unforgiveness prevents us from receiving the forgiveness we ourselves so desperately need—we've cut the God who forgives out of the equation.

This applies, by the way, even to withholding forgiveness from ourselves. "I'll never forgive myself" is an atheistic statement, because it appoints the self as ruler and judge.

A Concern for Relational Wholeness

Ruth Graham, wife of evangelist Billy Graham, was asked, "What is the secret to a lasting marriage?" Given the idealistic light in which we saw her husband, her answer surprised me.

"Forgiveness."

Jesus knows we have no shot at staying in relationship with one another without the power of forgiveness. He also knows unforgiveness hurts us more than the perpetrator. As Marianne Williamson famously put it, "Unforgiveness is like drinking poison yourself and waiting for the other person to die."

So it makes sense that Jesus, the Lover of our Souls, would include a deep concern for relational wholeness—with God, with each other, and with ourselves—into this petition.

BUT WHAT IF I CAN'T FORGIVE?

Maybe you've been treated so wrongly and been wounded so deeply that the idea of forgiving the perpetrator seems obscene. What should we do when forgiveness seems impossible?

Many people have experienced horrific harm and lasting trauma. Jesus knows this. He sees what happens and does not take it lightly. He knows it takes time to access painful memories and work through anger. Even after taking these steps we may still have ill will in our heart for the perpetrator. The inner sense of having truly forgiven someone can't be forced—it's a gift from God. Our part, after doing what we can to grieve the offense, is to take a step of faith to say, "I'm willing. I'm willing to be willing. I choose to release the person as best as I am able."

God will do something beautiful with whatever opening we give him. Forgiveness doesn't mean we place ourselves in harm's way or remain in toxic relationships. Rather, forgiveness is a journey toward abdicating the judgment seat and being released from the bondage of resentment.

Arriving at the ability to forgive someone is a process—sometimes a slow and painful one. But where I used to think it was something God demanded of us, I see now that it is something he longs to give us. So we pray the first half of the fifth petition, recognizing our deep need for right relationship. And then we pray the second half, giving God permission to cultivate forgiveness inside of us, however long it takes. As with all the other petitions, we're asking God to do the good and beautiful things that only he can do.

Suggested song: "Willing"
renovare.org/universesongs

LIVING INSIDE THE FIFTH PETITION

Consider praying through the Anglican liturgy for confession:

Most merciful God,
we confess that we have sinned against you
in thought, word, and deed,
by what we have done,
and by what we have left undone.
We have not loved you with our whole heart;
we have not loved our neighbors as ourselves.
We are truly sorry and we humbly repent.
For the sake of your Son Jesus Christ,
have mercy on us and forgive us;
that we may delight in your will,
and walk in your ways,
to the glory of your Name. Amen.

Then read Psalm 103:10–12 as assurance of forgiveness:

[The Lord] does not deal with us according to our sins,
nor repay us according to our iniquities.
For as the heavens are high above the earth,
so great is his steadfast love toward those who fear him;
as far as the east is from the west,
so far he removes our transgressions from us.

DAY SEVEN
PETITION SIX

And lead us not into temptation, but deliver us from evil.

This portion of the Lord's Prayer has given commentators the most fits over the centuries. Would God ever actually lead us into temptation, such that we need to ask him not to?

TESTS AND TEMPTATIONS[14]

Darrell Johnson helps clarify this seemingly confusing petition. He points out that *pierasmos*—the Greek word translated as "temptation" in Matthew 6:13—can also mean "test" or "trial." When translated as "temptation," it refers to a deliberate attempt to ensnare a person in something evil. But when the word is translated as "test," it refers to something positive—the way gold is tested by fire to be both evaluated and refined.

These two different meanings of *pierasmos* are seen in the first chapter of James. Verses 2–3 read, "My brothers and sisters, whenever you face trials of any kind, consider it nothing but joy, because you know that the testing of your faith produces endurance." This passage points to the truth that we usually experience the most growth through the hardest stretches.

In verse 13, James cautions, "No one, when tempted, should say, 'I am being tempted by God'; for God cannot be tempted by evil and he himself tempts no one." Here, using the very same

Greek word, James is making it clear that it is never God's intention to lead us into evil.

So why is *pierasmos* translated as "temptation" rather than "test" in Matthew 6:13? Perhaps because we're tempted to misread our trials to mean that God is no longer with us or for us. Satan took this tack in the wilderness. But Jesus was too thoroughly acquainted with his Father's goodness to fall for Satan's lie that God could not be trusted in a time of trial.

When trials inevitably come, Jesus teaches us to pray that Satan won't convince us that God has abandoned us. Johnson's paraphrase of Matthew 6:13 reads, "Father, as you lead us to the test, do not let the test become a temptation, but rescue us from the one who seeks to destroy our faith, and work in us the same confidence in you that Jesus has."[15]

We see again why the first petition is for the hallowing of God's name. Jesus knows the *only* thing that can defeat us is if we become permanently convinced that God is not good.

DELIVER US FROM EVIL

The final thing Jesus teaches us to ask for is deliverance from evil, which indicates that evil is real and we shouldn't underestimate it. There truly is an enemy who would love to devour us. Remember, this enemy's primary *modus operandi* is attempting to deceive us into thinking God cannot be trusted.

But if Jesus is realistic about evil, he is also utterly confident about its defeat. He knows we are not in some dualistic battle where good and evil are equal opponents and the outcome is uncertain. In fact, nothing could be further from the truth.

As a church kid, I loved the special Sundays when missionaries on furlough brought reports. There is one visit I've never forgotten.[16]

The missionary couple was stationed in what appeared in photos to be a particularly steamy jungle. One day, they told us, an enormous snake—much longer than a man—slithered its way through their front door and into the kitchen of their simple home. Terrified, they ran outside and searched frantically for a local who might know what to do. A machete-wielding neighbor came to the rescue, calmly marching into their house and decapitating the snake with one clean chop.

The neighbor reemerged triumphant and assured the missionaries that the reptile had been defeated. But there was a catch, he warned: It was going to take a while for the snake to realize it was dead.

A snake's neurology and blood flow are such that it can take considerable time for it to stop moving even after decapitation. For the next several hours, the missionaries were forced to wait outside while the snake thrashed about, smashing furniture and flailing against walls and windows, wreaking havoc until its body finally understood that it no longer had a head.

Sweating in the heat, they felt frustrated but also grateful that the snake's rampage wouldn't last forever. At some point they had a mutual epiphany.

I leaned in with the rest of the congregation, queasy and fascinated. "Do you see it?" asked the husband. "Satan is a lot like that big old snake. He's already been defeated. He just doesn't know it yet. In the meantime, he's going to do some damage. But never forget that he's a goner."

That story is a picture of the universe. We are in the thrashing time, a season characterized by our capacity to do violence to each other and ourselves. The temptation is to despair. We have to remember, though, that it won't last forever. Jesus has already crushed the serpent's head.

There is still a waiting. In some cases, the redemption and healing Jesus obtained for us on the cross may not come in fullness until we are face-to-face with our Victor—but come it will. Guaranteed.

One wondrous mystery is that although the end of the story has already been determined, God is still using us to write it. We have the dignity of causality. Because Jesus lives in us through his Spirit, we are called not just to anticipate the ultimate reign of his kingdom, but also to play a part in bringing it to fruition.

And so we live inside the prayer Jesus taught us. We affirm that the kingdom is at hand. We sign up for the revolution.

We ask God to do what only he can do—and to do it in and through us, even now.

Suggested song: "The Last Word (Love Was Here First)"
renovare.org/universesongs

The Lord's Prayer
(Dallas Willard Paraphrase)

Dear Father, always near us,
may your name be treasured and loved,
may your rule be completed in us—
may your will be done here on earth
in just the way it is done in heaven.

Give us today the things we need today,
and forgive us our sins and impositions on you
as we are forgiving all who in any way offend us.

Please don't put us through trials,
but deliver us from everything bad.

Because you are the one in charge,
and you have all the power,
and the glory too is all yours—forever—
which is just the way we want it!

AMEN (Whoopie!)

LIVING INSIDE THE SIXTH PETITION

Do you face a temptation to doubt God's goodness and the fact that he is with you and for you? As you pray for deliverance from evil and oppression, "pray back" God's character as the Deliverer:

- the One who freed Israel from Egyptian captivity
- the One who welcomed outcasts and healed the sick, freeing them from estrangement and illness
- the One who delivered us from death and decay on the cross

Use this last day inside the Lord's Prayer to gather up the threads of all that you've explored throughout the journey. Be sure to journal anything you've heard from God, as well as the questions and petitions that remain.

ENDNOTES

1. N. T. Wright, *The Lord and His Prayer* (Grand Rapids: Eerdmans, 2014), 7.
2. Darrell W. Johnson, *Fifty-Seven Words That Change the World* (Vancouver, BC: Regent College Publishing, 2005), 14. The phrase "dignity of causality" comes from Blaise Pascal, as quoted by Johnson.
3. Johnson, *Fifty-Seven Words*, 15.
4. I was introduced to the Crab Nebula in Annie Dillard's essay "Total Eclipse," which can be found in *Teaching a Stone to Talk* (New York: Harper & Roe, 1982), 9-28.
5. Dallas Willard, *The Divine Conspiracy: Rediscovering Our Hidden Life in God* (San Francisco: HarperSanFrancisco, 1998), 255.
6. Ibid., 256.
7. Baxter Kruger, "Theology: Perichor . . . what?" https://archive.gci.org/articles/perichor-what/.
8. Wright, *The Lord and His Prayer*, 17.
9. This reflection is adapted from Johnson, *Fifty-Seven Words*, 39.
10. Willard, *Divine Conspiracy*, 25.
11. Ibid., 21.
12. Parts of this story are adapted from my article "You Probably Won't Be Sent to Egypt," originally published in the July 2013 issue of *Christianity Today*.
13. The Palms Up, Palms Down Prayer is described by Richard Foster in *Celebration of Discipline* (San Francisco: HarperOne), 30-31.
14. Parts of this section are from my article "Temptation on Trial," in the January/February 2018 edition of *Faith Today*.
15. Johnson, *Fifty-Seven Words*, 100.
16. Parts of this story are adapted from my article "Satan's a Goner," originally published in the February 2011 issue of *Christianity Today*.

For a free digital version of this booklet and other spiritual formation resources, visit **renovare.org**